# JACK, ZACK AND MACK

Written by Charlotte Raby

Illustrated by Caroline Romanet

Jack, Zack and Mack were friends.
They had loads of fun doing tricks.

Zack jumped up at Jack as
he went down the road.

Mack croaked like a mad toad.
He terrified Zack.

Zack fell over and got soaked.
It was fun tricking Zack!

6

Mack hid in an oak tree.
He spied on Jack and Zack.

Jack and Zack waited.

They were very fed up.

"Come on, Mack," they moaned.

Zack and Jack had a picnic.
Mack wanted to get down.

"Oh no!" he groaned. "I am stuck!"
It was no fun tricking Jack and Zack!

Zack and Jack spied Mack.

He needed help, so they coaxed him down.

And from then on, the three friends stopped doing tricks!